D1266488

Native
American
Peoples

COMANCHE

D. L. Birchfield

Gareth Stevens Publishing
A WORLD ALMANAC EDUCATION GROUP COMPANY

Please visit our web site at: www.garethstevens.com
For a free color catalog describing Gareth Stevens Publishing's list of high-quality books and multimedia programs, call 1-800-542-2595 (USA) or 1-800-387-3178 (Canada). Gareth Stevens Publishing's fax: (414) 332-3567.

Library of Congress Cataloging-in-Publication Data

Birchfield, D. L., 1948-
    Comanche / by D. L. Birchfield.
      p. cm. — (Native American peoples)
    Summary: A discussion of the history, culture, and contemporary life of the Comanche Indians.
    Includes bibliographical references and index.
    ISBN 0-8368-3702-9 (lib. bdg.)
    1. Comanche Indians—Juvenile literature. [1. Comanche Indians. 2. Indians of North America—Great Plains.] I. Title. II. Series.
    E99.C85B57   2003
    978.004'9745—dc21   2003045709

First published in 2004 by
Gareth Stevens Publishing
A World Almanac Education Group Company
330 West Olive Street, Suite 100
Milwaukee, WI 53212 USA

Copyright © 2004 by Gareth Stevens Publishing.

Produced by Discovery Books
Project editor: Valerie J. Weber
Designer and page production: Sabine Beaupré
Photo researcher: Rachel Tisdale
Native American consultant: Robert J. Conley, M.A., Former Director of Native American Studies at Morningside College and Montana State University
Maps and diagrams: Stefan Chabluk
Gareth Stevens editorial direction: Mark Sachner
Gareth Stevens art direction: Tammy Gruenewald
Gareth Stevens production: Beth Meinholz and Jessica L. Yanke

Photo credits: Native Stock: cover, pp. 13, 14, 15 (both), 17, 18 (both), 19 (both), 20, 21, 24, 26 (both), 27; Peter Newark's American Pictures: pp. 5, 6, 9, 10; North Wind Picture Archives: pp. 7, 11 (top); Corbis: pp. 11 (bottom), 12, 16 (both), 23. 25; AP/Wide World Photos: p. 22.

Printed in the United States of America

1 2 3 4 5 6 7 8 9 07 06 05 04 03

Cover caption: Two young Comanche men in competition powwow dress. At competition powwows, dancers compete for prizes.

Contents

Words that appear in the glossary are printed in
boldface type the first time they appear in the text.

Origins

As the red areas indicate, the Comanches migrated from Wyoming to the southern Great Plains. By the 1800s, they controlled much of present-day Kansas, Oklahoma, and Texas (as shown in violet).

Comanche Country

The Comanches are a North American Native people with close to ten thousand tribal members. Many live near the Comanche **Nation** tribal headquarters in southwestern Oklahoma, while others live throughout North America.

Historically, Comanches were lords of the southern Great Plains, dominating a huge area from southern Kansas to central Texas and from eastern New Mexico to central Oklahoma. Their power was felt deep into Mexico, where ranchers feared their lightning-quick raids for cattle and horses.

How the Comanches Arrived

Comanche origin stories tell of a time when great swirling winds from the four directions kicked up dust in a giant storm. The wind created a people with the power of storms and the strength of the earth from which they had been made.

No one knows for sure how long Comanches and other Indians have been in North America or how they might have first arrived here. For years, many scholars and scientists have believed that Comanches and all other Indians came to North America from Asia over a landmass across the Bering Strait during the last Ice

Photographed in 1892, these two young Comanche girls are wearing traditional clothing.

Age. Recent discoveries of older sites have prompted scholars to develop other theories about how Indians arrived on the continent. Perhaps they sailed by boat from Asia and traveled across South, Central, and North America on foot.

The name *Comanche* might be of Spanish origin, from *camino ancho,* meaning "the broad trail," referring to the Comanche raiding trails. The Comanche name for themselves is *Nerm* (sometimes *Neum, Nimenim,* or *Nununuh*), meaning "people of people" or "the people."

Comanche Words

The Comanche language is part of the Shoshonean language family. Most of the other tribes that speak Shoshonean languages (such as the Bannocks, Paiutes, Shoshones, and Utes) live in the northern Rocky Mountains or the Great Basin desert country of Nevada.

Comanche	Pronunciation	English
haa	hah	yes
ke	kay	no
kutu	koo-too	yesterday
tosa	tow-sah	white
hini	hee-nee	what?
hubi	hoo-bee	woman
toya	tow-yah	mountain
aho	ah-hoe	hello
kuhma	koo-mah	man

History

The Historic Migration

Comanches once lived in the northern Rocky Mountains in central Wyoming. They survived mostly by hunting deer and elk on foot, as they had for hundreds of years. Once they acquired horses in the late 1600s, however, the Comanches started moving to the southern Great Plains, and their lives changed quickly and dramatically. They became masters at hunting the huge southern buffalo herds.

Their migration south also changed the lives of many other people, both Indians and Europeans. By the early 1700s, the Spanish, who had entered the Southwest in the mid-1500s, began encountering Comanches in what is now southeastern Colorado.

Artist George Catlin visited a Comanche village in Texas in the 1830s and made this painting. The women on the right are preparing a buffalo hide.

Trying to Stop the Comanche Tide

The Comanche migration alarmed the Spanish because it threatened to disrupt Indian relations in New Mexico. The Spanish had made friends with the Plains Apaches, but now that tribe was in danger of being driven off the southern Great Plains by the Comanches.

Artist Frederick Remington painted this Comanche man on horseback in the nineteenth century. A painter and sculptor, Remington captured aspects of Native American life, traveling all over the West.

The Plains Apaches asked for help from the Spanish, who built a fort in the Plains Apache country to defend their friends. Nothing could stop the Comanches, however, who numbered in the thousands.

Sometime about 1724, many different bands of Plains Apaches came together to make one last desperate effort to hold back the Comanches. They fought a great battle, but the Comanches won, driving the Plains Apaches into the mountains of New Mexico. By the mid-1700s, the Comanches had taken control of the southern Great Plains all the way to central Texas.

An Abandoned Fort

In the early 1700s, the Spanish in New Mexico made great efforts to try to help their friends, the Plains Apaches, fight against the Comanche invasion. At great expense, the Spanish built a fort in present-day southeastern Colorado, beside the largest village of Plains Apaches, and stationed many soldiers there. (The fort, village, and Apache band all took the same name — El Quartelejo.) When an Apache got sick and died, however, the tribe moved its village many miles away because the Apaches always moved to a new place when someone died. The Spanish, unable to pick up their fort and move with them, had to give up trying to help their friends.

The Spanish Colonial Era

During the mid-1700s, the Comanches made life miserable for the Spanish in New Mexico and Texas. There were so many Comanches — and so few Spanish soldiers — that Comanches raided the Spanish ranches at will, stealing horses by the thousands. Comanches soon became rich by trading the animals to other tribes farther north.

Politics on the Plains

This changed, however, in 1787 when the Comanches became military allies of the Spanish in New Mexico and a great peace changed life for everyone in the region. The Comanches helped the Spanish fight the Apaches, the former allies of the Spanish who had been forced into raiding Spanish cattle herds after they had lost the buffalo plains to the Comanches. By 1790, the Spanish and Comanches were able to make almost all the Apaches stop raiding and settle near Spanish missions.

Iron Shirt

In 1787, Iron Shirt, a great military leader, was chief of the Comanches on the buffalo plains of eastern New Mexico. He convinced his people to make peace with the Spanish in New Mexico, which brought many advantages to the Comanches. They were then able to trade their buffalo meat and buffalo robes with the Spanish and the Pueblo Indians in New Mexico. The goods they received in exchange made life easier for the Comanches. These goods included Pueblo pottery and farm products, such as corn and beans, as well as Spanish trade goods, such as metal pots, guns, and ammunition.

That peace between the Spanish and the Comanches ended, however, during the chaos of the Mexican Revolution from 1810 to 1820. After Mexico won its independence from Spain in 1820, the Comanches considered their **alliance** over and went back to raiding whenever they wanted.

In 1848, the United States defeated Mexico in a war and acquired New Mexico as a territory. Texas had already gained its independence from Mexico in 1835 and had become a U.S. state in 1845. Comanches now faced a new and much stronger military power for control of the southern Great Plains — the United States.

Artist George Catlin was an eyewitness when Comanches greeted a U.S. cavalry troop on the Great Plains in 1835. Catlin sketched this drawing of their meeting.

Trying to Control the Comanches

The first attempt by the United States to establish its authority in the region was mostly **defensive**. The U.S. Army built a line of forts across the Texas frontier, hoping to restrict the Comanches' movements. The forts, however, did little to stop the Indians from doing as they pleased; the Comanches traveled throughout the region as they always had.

After the **Civil War** (1861–1865), the U.S. Army became more aggressive. Large armies defeated some Comanche bands, forcing them to move to a reservation under the **Treaty** of Medicine Lodge of 1867. However, the U.S. government did not provide food as it had promised in the treaty, so many of those Comanches rejoined their tribe on the Plains.

The Texas Rangers

In 1858, a special "Frontier Battalion" of soldiers called the Texas Rangers began making surprise attacks on Comanche villages outside the state of Texas, killing men, women, and children. The Texas Rangers taught the U.S. Army that Comanches could be attacked deep in their homeland, a lesson that the army was quick to learn and apply.

Carl von Iwonski painted *Terry's Texas Rangers* in 1845. The Texas Rangers were formed specifically to hunt down Indians, whether they lived in Texas or not.

These Indians require to be soundly whipped, and the ringleaders . . . hung, their ponies killed, and such destruction of their property as will make them very poor.

U.S. General William Sherman, 1868

The War on the Plains

The end came swiftly for the Comanches. In 1874, in the Red River War, the U.S. Army launched a massive **campaign**, with many soldiers coming from forts in all directions. The soldiers had cannons and an early kind of machine gun, called a Gatling gun, that could fire four

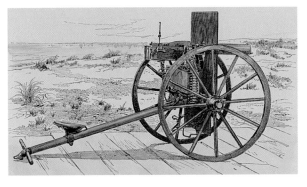

This photo shows an early type of army machine gun in the 1880s, known generally as a Gatling gun. This model was called a Maxim field gun.

hundred shots a minute. The Comanches ran for their lives; the soldiers then burned their abandoned villages. At Palo Duro Canyon in the Texas Panhandle, the soldiers also shot and killed more than one thousand captured Comanche horses.

As winter set in, the Comanches were left with nothing. Starving and freezing, they had little choice but to go to the forts and give themselves up. By the spring of 1875, virtually all of the Comanches had surrendered. On the southern Great Plains, American hide hunters soon killed the last remaining buffaloes on which the Comanches had depended. The old Comanche way of life ended, and the **reservation** era began.

Now a state park, Palo Duro Canyon in the Texas Panhandle, a place of great beauty, was a favorite site for Comanche villages.

On July 29, 1901, about thirty thousand people gathered to watch settlers trying to win their own section of Comanche lands in a lottery. The Comanches could only watch helplessly as most of their land was given to white settlers.

Reservation Life

Perhaps no other Indian people were less suited to reservation life than the Comanches. Long accustomed to riding free across the Plains, they suddenly found themselves on foot in present-day southwestern Oklahoma.

Their reservation, near the rocky and dry Wichita Mountains, was not well suited to farming, but the U.S. forced them to try to become farmers. Their children were taken from them and sent away to **boarding schools**.

Loss of the Land

U.S. treaties promised that Comanches would have their reservation forever, but by the late nineteenth century, land-hungry whites demanded the Comanche reservation land. In 1892, Congress forced the Comanches to accept individual ownership of small farms, called **allotments**, and sold the rest of the Comanche land to whites.

In 1907, Comanches were forced to become citizens of the new state of Oklahoma, and the U.S. government argued that the Comanche Nation no longer existed. Under the Indian Reorganization Act in 1934, however, the Comanches were allowed to form a joint business committee with the Kiowas and Kiowa-Apaches. That was the only form of government the Comanches had until their nation was allowed to organize a new government in 1963.

Throughout most of the twentieth century, the United States government and the state of Oklahoma tried to suppress Comanche **culture**, including religion, and to force Comanches to **assimilate** and become more like white people. Comanches would not have their own government again until late in the twentieth century. They still do not have all their land back.

Quanah Parker

Quanah Parker (1845–1911) was the son of a Comanche war chief and a white woman who had been captured by the Comanches. He too became a famous war chief and by 1890 was head of all the Comanche bands. On the reservation, he learned English quickly and helped the tribe raise money by leasing grazing land to whites. He was a judge on an Indian criminal court until the U.S. government removed him when it found out he had five Comanche wives. He managed his land and money so well that he became an influential leader of Indians on national issues.

Quanah Parker with two of his wives. The government refused to respect traditional Comanche marriages.

Traditional Way of Life

A small buffalo herd near the Wichita Mountains in southwestern Oklahoma. Buffalo herds once roamed the southern Great Plains in huge numbers.

Traditional Economy

The Comanche traditional **economy** was based on buffaloes and horses. The great herds of buffalo on the southern Great Plains provided for almost all the Comanches' needs. Buffalo sinews, the tough, stringy tendons, made excellent bowstrings. Boiled down to make glue, even the buffalo hooves were put to use.

Buffalo meat provided more than fresh food. It could also be stored for winter food or trail food. This was done by cutting it into thin strips, salting it, and hanging it in the sun to remove most of the moisture. The dried meat was also pounded and mixed with nuts and berries to make a tasty, lightweight trail food known as pemmican.

Left: This outdoor museum display allows visitors to see a teepee. At the right is a travois, a horse-drawn sled for moving heavy items.
Right: This museum display shows how Comanches prepared buffalo meat. The rack at the left is holding strips of meat for drying into buffalo jerky.

While the hides supplied clothing and warm winter blankets, tepees made of buffalo hides gave the Comanches highly mobile homes. The long, slender pine poles that held up the tepee became the frame of a long sled, called a travois, when they moved. Carrying the buffalo hides that covered the tepees, the travois was dragged behind a horse.

Buffalo meat and hides also gave the Comanches valuable items for trade with other people, especially with the Spanish and the Pueblo Indians of New Mexico.

Superb Horse Traders

Comanches became the greatest horse dealers in North American history. They had an endless supply of horses, stealing them by the thousands on raids in Texas and deep into Mexico. The Comanches traded the horses to tribes farther north on the Great Plains, becoming the main source of supply for a traffic that kept Indian tribes well mounted all the way to Canada.

The practice of stealing horses has prevailed very much to the great disquiet of the citizens of the United States. . . . It is therefore agreed to that it shall be put an entire stop to on both sides.

U.S. treaty with the Comanches, 1848

Comanche war chief Mow-wi (Hand Shaker) once led the Kwahada (Antelope) band of Comanches.

An 1872 photo of Comanche leader Astlavi (also known as Milky Way or Bird Chief). He was a leader of the Penateka (Honey Eaters) band.

Comancheros

Comancheros were Mexicans and Americans who were engaged in a very dangerous line of work — conducting illegal trade with the Comanches. During the era of the Indian wars in the nineteenth century, the Comancheros operated out of New Mexico, driving wagons filled with trade goods far out onto the Plains to find the Comanches. The Comanches depended on the Comancheros for guns, ammunition, and other goods when they were at war and could not get those things from other sources. When Comanches were forced to accept reservation life, the Comanchero trade ended.

From the mid-1700s to the mid-1800s, Comanches enjoyed a position of power and wealth that made them one of the most successful Native American groups in history. It made the change to reservation life especially difficult for a proud people who had achieved so much.

Tribal Divisions

Comanches were never a unified political nation until after they were forced to accept reservation life. Over the past several hundred years, they have sometimes had as few as three tribal divisions and sometimes as many as twelve. Each one operated as an independent unit, with different territory on the buffalo plains. By the mid-nineteenth century, they had come to have six tribal divisions: Kwahada (Antelope), Nokoni (Wanderers), Penateka (Honey Eaters), Tenema (Downstream People), Kotsoteka (Buffalo Eaters), and Yamparika (Root Eaters).

Historically, Comanches were remarkable for their success at avoiding the **temptations** of alcohol. Each warrior society was also capable of organized, coordinated military efforts, unlike many other Plains tribes, where each Indian was often his own boss. This difference made it possible for Comanche chiefs to plan military efforts almost like army generals.

A museum display of traditional Comanche clothing. The shirt is made of buckskin.

Comanches and Kiowas

In about 1790, the Comanches entered into a historic peace with the Kiowas that has never been broken. The two tribes traveled together, hunted together, and fought together against common enemies.

The two tribes could not have been more different however. The Kiowas continually complained to the Comanches about being too hot-headed, too rash, and too ready to fly off the handle in an instant. The Comanches complained to the Kiowas that they would talk a problem to death rather than ever do anything about it. Together, they balanced one another's natural tendencies and maintained a remarkable partnership that controlled a huge expanse of land for a long time.

Traditional Games

Comanches are a people who love to play games. One of their favorites is a dice game, made with dice carved from pieces of bone.

These carved pieces of bone are dice crafted by Comanches. They were used in very popular gambling games.

They also show great skill at their favorite game, the Indian hand game, which is popular among most Plains tribes. The hand game is a team sport. Seated in a row across from a rival team, team members rapidly pass a small item, often a bone, button, or bullet, from hand to hand. When the action stops, the rival team must guess which person actually holds the item. Comanches today can play the game for hours. In the old days, it provided entertainment on many cold days and nights in the winter tepees. Frequently, the game involved betting virtually everything valuable that team members owned.

An Artistic People

Comanche crafts are some of the most beautiful of the Plains Indians' art. Comanches excelled at making parfleches, finely crafted storage containers made of tanned elk hide. Colored with natural dyes and decorated with beadwork and porcupine quills, some are beautiful works of art.

Comanche parfleches were used for storing and transporting food and other items. Many Native groups produced beautifully designed parfleches.

A museum display of moccasins. Note the fine beadwork, carefully crafted by Comanche women.

Shirts, dresses, and moccasins made from deer and elk hides were also finely crafted and beautifully decorated. Comanches take pride in their appearance, and the women fashioned clothing that was both functional and attractive.

Where Did the Museum Get That?

Many of the historic Comanche craft items in museums and private collections were stolen from families during the period when Comanches were being forced to accept reservation life. During that era, many Americans believed that Indians had no rights. Soldiers stole items. Indian agents and missionaries stole items. Traditional clothing worn by Comanche children when they were sent to boarding schools was taken away from them and not returned. Many of those items ended up in museums. Today, Comanches and other Indians are demanding their things be returned to them.

Made from tiny beads, this medallion necklace is displayed at the Oklahoma Natural History Museum.

A buffalo skull painted for ceremonial use.

Beliefs

Comanche culture is deeply religious. Traditional Comanches believe in an afterlife and revere the Great Spirit. They engage in periods of fasting and seek **visions** to help guide them in life. Traditional Comanches had great confidence in the power of **medicine men** to cure illness, help interpret dreams, and help guide the nation in times of crisis.

A Misleading Medicine Man

In 1874, however, a young Comanche medicine man, Isatai, told people he had **supernatural** powers. He gained a large following, including war chief Quanah Parker. Isatai said that if the Comanches held a Sun Dance, they would be safe from the bullets of the American hide hunters who were killing all the buffaloes.

In June 1874, the Comanches held the Sun Dance, which is a ceremony of dedication to the welfare of the tribe. After the ceremony, Isatai and Quanah Parker led a large force of Comanches in an attack on a small group of buffalo-hide hunters at Adobe Walls, Texas. When the buffalo-hide hunters killed several Comanches at great distances with their new high-powered buffalo guns, the Natives withdrew, and Isatai lost his following. After these events, Comanche medicine men lost their influence in the tribe. Quanah Parker and most of the other Comanche leaders never believed in their powers again.

The Native American Church

A museum display of fans and rattles used in ceremonies of the Native American Church.

Beginning in the 1880s, Quanah Parker became a strong supporter of using peyote, a drug that comes from the cactus plant, in Indian religious ceremonies that the Comanches learned from the Lipan Apaches. He traveled widely to Indian communities across North America, helping found what later came to be officially called the Native American Church. Many Comanches joined this church in the early 1900s. For most of the twentieth century, the U.S. government and the various states **persecuted** members of the Native American Church with harsh drug laws. Today, members of the church are no longer subject to those laws.

Today

Arguments over the use of Native Americans as symbols for sports teams often focus on Chief Illiniwek, the University of Illinois's mascot.

Literature and the Arts

Comanches have been leaders in expressing modern-day Native American issues and concerns to non-Indians. Comanche writer Cornel Pewewardy is one of the most active Indian writers trying to get Americans to stop using Indians as **mascots** for sports teams. His articles on that issue have appeared in many publications. He has also had a distinguished career in education, becoming the youngest school principal on the Navajo Reservation. In 1991, the National Indian Education Association named him Indian Educator of the Year for his work with an Indian school in Minnesota; he is currently an English professor at the University of Kansas. A performing artist of traditional Comanche flute music, Pewewardy has recorded a number of compact discs.

Paul Chaat Smith coauthored one of the most influential books about the **American Indian Movement** (AIM) of the late 1960s and early 1970s. His book, *Like a Hurricane*, describes how AIM members staged protests in the United States that brought worldwide attention to the poverty and hopelessness on many reservations. The **media** attention caused Congress to change many laws and to allow Indians more religious freedom and a chance to have better lives.

Comanche poet Juanita Pahdopony has been an inspiration to young Comanche writers. She has helped conduct many workshops where young Indians learn how to get their poetry and other writing published. She teaches at the Comanche Nation tribal college in Lawton, Oklahoma.

The Comanche Nation

For nearly a hundred years after the Medicine Lodge Treaty of 1867, the Comanches were formally joined with the Kiowa and Kiowa-Apache tribes. During much of the twentieth century, they conducted their affairs with a joint business committee made up of representatives of all three tribes.

LaDonna Harris

An influential leader, Comanche writer LaDonna Harris (born in 1931) publishes articles about how Comanches and other tribes can start businesses and create jobs for their people. She grew up among her people and spoke only the Comanche language until she started school. In 1965, she founded an organization called Oklahomans for Indian Opportunity that helps Indian people have better lives.

LaDonna Harris meets with an Indian woman in 1973. Harris has been one of the most active national leaders for Indian people, opposing discrimination in housing and other areas.

In recent centuries, Comanches have been a people on the move, migrating from the northern Rocky Mountains to the southern Great Plains. The Comanche Nations' headquarters is now near Lawton, Oklahoma.

In 1963, however, the Comanches organized the Comanche Nation of Oklahoma. Their tribal headquarters is located north of the small city of Lawton, near the Wichita Mountains of southwestern Oklahoma.

Under the leadership of Wallace Coffee, Jr., as tribal chairman, the Comanches successfully issued their own license plates for tribal members' cars, despite the protests of the state of Oklahoma. They have also opened a bingo operation, joined with the Kiowas and Kiowa-Apaches in developing a water recreation park, and started their own tribally controlled college.

Medicine Bluff Creek in the Comanche homeland near the Wichita Mountains of southwestern Oklahoma.

Ever since the allotment of tribal land was completed in 1906, the Comanches have lived scattered throughout their former reservation, mixed in with the general rural population of southwestern Oklahoma. Many are farmers and ranchers or live in the small towns in the region. Many others are scattered throughout the continent, pursuing the same kind of careers as other Americans. Most Comanche children now attend the public schools in Oklahoma. Today, their activities and interests are very similar to those of other children in Oklahoma.

In modern times, Chief Wallace Coffey continued the great tradition of leadership of his people displayed by Comanche chiefs of past eras.

～Comanche Nation Buffalo Herd ～

Of all the recent changes in the Comanche Nation, perhaps none is more symbolic or more meaningful for the people than the beginning, in 2001, of a Comanche Nation buffalo herd. The herd began with five animals, but there are plans to increase the size of the herd quickly. Though the tribe owns little pasture, the Comanches plan to farm out the buffaloes to tribal members who will share the resulting calves with the tribe. Buffalo meat contains a natural substance that fights **diabetes**, a disease from which many Indians suffer. Comanches hope soon to be able to supply buffalo meat to all tribal elders and eventually to all tribal members.

Young Comanches demonstrate a competition powwow dance for visitors to Indian City, USA, a popular tourist attraction near Anadarko, Oklahoma.

A Culture Grows Stronger

Over the last few decades, Comanches have been experiencing a cultural **revival**. After a century of intense attempts by the U.S. government to make them give up their Indian ways and blend into the larger European-American culture, Comanches are now being allowed to publicly embrace their traditions again. It is a huge change from one hundred years ago, when most Americans assumed that both the Comanche people and their culture would disappear forever.

In 1972, one of their old warrior societies, the Little Pony Society, was revived to honor returning Comanche Vietnam War veterans. In 1976, the Yamparika division of the Comanches revived their Black Knives Society.

Modern-day Comanche Warrior Society members in traditional dress gather for a tribal meeting in southwestern Oklahoma.

26

Once made up of some of the best warriors in the nation, those societies had been inactive for nearly a century.

Other Comanche societies have become active again, including the Comanche Gourd Society and the Comanche War Dance Society. The War Dance Society was recently given permission by the Osage Nation to perform the Osage Heluska Society's Straight War Dance, an honor rarely given to another Indian nation.

Princess competitions are popular events in many tribes in Oklahoma, and this Comanche girl has just won the contest.

Looking to the Future

While many Comanches are reestablishing their cultural roots, many are also active leaders in the business, professional, and political life of Oklahoma. Comanches work as doctors, lawyers, and managers; some are teachers, school administrators, and college professors. The Comanches have also produced great poets and scholars.

The most valuable resource of the Comanche Nation is its people. They have endured enormous hardships and have survived to enter the twenty-first century with renewed hope for the future.

Comanche Homecoming

An annual event, the Comanche Homecoming takes place in mid-July at Walters, a small town in southwestern Oklahoma. The powwow was started in 1952 to honor returning Comanche Korean War veterans and has been continued since then as the homecoming powwow. During Homecoming, Comanches camp together, renew old friendships, and visit with relatives.

Time Line

late 1600s	Comanches begin leaving Wyoming for southern Great Plains.
1720s	Spanish in New Mexico try helping friendly Plains Apaches hold back Comanches from driving Apaches off the Plains.
about 1724	Apaches lose big battle with Comanches, who take control of the southern Great Plains.
1787	Comanche leader Iron Shirt makes historic peace with the Spanish in New Mexico.
late 1780s	Comanche warriors join Spanish soldiers and Navajo warriors in tracking down hostile Apaches and forcing them to live near Spanish missions, bringing a short era of peace to the region.
1790	Comanches enter into historic peace with the Kiowa tribe.
1810–20	Long, bloody Mexican Revolution brings chaos to the Southwest; Indian peace breaks down.
1835	First Comanche treaty with United States; Texans fight Comanches as Texas ranchers move deeper into their homeland.
1840	Comanches and Kiowas enter into historic peace with the Cheyennes, become allies in wars with United States.
1848	United States gains New Mexico as a U.S. territory.
1858	Texas Rangers begin attacking Comanches outside of Texas.
1867	Treaty of Medicine Lodge establishes Comanche reservation.
1892	Congress forces Comanches to accept allotments.
1918	Native American Church officially founded.
1941–45	Comanches in U.S. Signal Corps use a signal code based on the Comanche language in World War II.
1963	Comanches establish Comanche Nation of Oklahoma.
1990s	Comanches open a bingo operation; join with Kiowas and Kiowas-Apaches to open a water recreation park.
2001	Comanches begin raising tribal buffalo herd.

Glossary

alliance: an agreement between two or more groups to work together.

allotment: forcing Indians to accept individual ownership of small farms, rather than all Indian land being owned by the tribe as a whole.

American Indian Movement: an organization of Indians that tries to get the U.S. government to honor its treaties with Native Americans.

assimilate: to force one group to adopt the culture — the language, lifestyle, and values — of another.

boarding school: a place where children must live at the school.

campaign: large-scale army movements to attack.

Civil War: 1861 to 1865 war between northern and southern states.

culture: arts, beliefs, and customs that make up a people's way of life.

defensive: guarding or protecting against attack.

diabetes: disease in which there is too much sugar in someone's blood.

economy: how people make a living, how they feed themselves and provide for their other needs.

mascots: persons or animals adopted as good-luck symbols for teams.

media: television, newspapers, and other forms of communication.

medicine men: spiritual or religious leaders.

nation: people who have their own customs, laws, and land separate from other nations or peoples.

persecute: to punish for a belief or activity.

reservation: land set aside by the U.S. government for one or more specific Indian tribes to live on.

revival: an act of giving new strength; a renewal.

supernatural: beyond the natural world.

temptations: strong appeal.

treaty: an agreement among two or more nations.

visions: things seen or experienced that are not from this world but the supernatural one; they resemble dreams, but the person is awake.

More Resources

Web Sites:

http://www.texasindians.com/comanche.htm Click down this page to find out more about Comanches and their ways. Site includes several maps.

http://www.anthro.mankato.msus.edu/cultural/northamerica/comanche.html Information on the Comanche lifestyle.

Videos:

America's Great Indian Leaders. Questar, 2002.

The War against the Indians: The Dispossessed. Madarcy Records, 1995.

500 Nations. Warner Home Video, 1995.

Books:

Alter, Judy. *The Comanches.* Franklin Watts, 1994.

Bial, Raymond. *The Comanche* (Lifeways). Marshall Cavendish, 2000.

Lodge, Sally. *The Comanche* (Native American People). Rourke Publications, 1992.

Marrin, Albert. *Plains Warrior: Chief Quanah Parker and the Comanches.* Atheneum Books for Young Readers, 1996.

Mooney, Martin J. *The Comanche Indians* (Junior Library of American Indians). Chelsea House, 1993.

Schwartz, Michael. *LaDonna Harris* (Contemporary Biographies). Raintree Steck-Vaughn, 1997.

Things to Think About and Do

Eyewitness To History

Pretend you are a U.S. Army scout in 1835 on the Great Plains. You are on a hilltop waiting while a big buffalo herd of hundreds of thousands of animals is passing by. Write a short letter home telling your relatives what you are seeing.

You Are There

Pretend you are a newspaper reporter in 1870 with a group of American buffalo hunters. Write a short news story about what they are doing and what impact that is having on the Comanche way of life.

Faraway Friends

Pretend you are a farm boy or girl in Pennsylvania in 1890. The Indian boarding school nearby has given your father a Comanche boy to work on the family farm for the summer. He doesn't know very much English, isn't used to American food, is very homesick for his relatives, and sleeps in your father's barn with your pony. Write a short fiction story about working with him that summer.

Design a Parfleche

Look at the picture of the Comanche parfleche on page 18. Using a colorful pattern, design your own parfleche.

Index